Rock You Tonight

Written by

Emily Roussell,

Illustration and Book Design by

Chris Cooley,

Dream Big Publishing, CMCreative Design

Rock You Tonight

Published by Dream Big Publishing LLC

PO Box 11009

State College, PA 16805

www.emilyroussell.com

Illustration and Book Design by Chris Cooley

CMCreative Design
www.cmcreativedesign.com

Hard Cover ISBN: 978-0-9828055-0-3

Library of Congress Control Number: 2010930595

Signature Book Printing, Inc
www.sbpbooks.com
First printing, February 2011
Printed in the United States of America

To my babies, Peter and Grace

and any others who may bless our home,
this book is truly by you and for you. May you always know
and feel the love of those quiet nights when we just held
you and rocked.

To my wonderful husband, Mike,

and all those around me who encouraged me to see this
project through to completion. Thank you for your belief!

To Chris, my illustrator,

whose amazing talents and dedication truly
brought the story to life.

Time for bed

and to rest your sweet head...

I quickly kiss you, hug you
and wrap you up tight,
wishing for more time
to rock you tonight.

Soft lullaby music
warmly fills the room,
but Mommy's thoughts
start to zoom.

For even after
I've laid you down,
Mommy must begin
to run around.

Can't stop to rest,
there's so much to do:
cleaning, laundry,
and all those dishes too.

There's a mountain of paperwork,
I owe a call to a friend,
and so much more
before this night's end.

And don't forget
Mommy gets tired too;
there's only so much
this super-woman can do.

But as I move toward your crib
I can't help but linger -
your tiny hand
has wrapped around my finger.

A smile crosses your lips
as your eyes open once more.
How could I have thought of this
as just another chore?

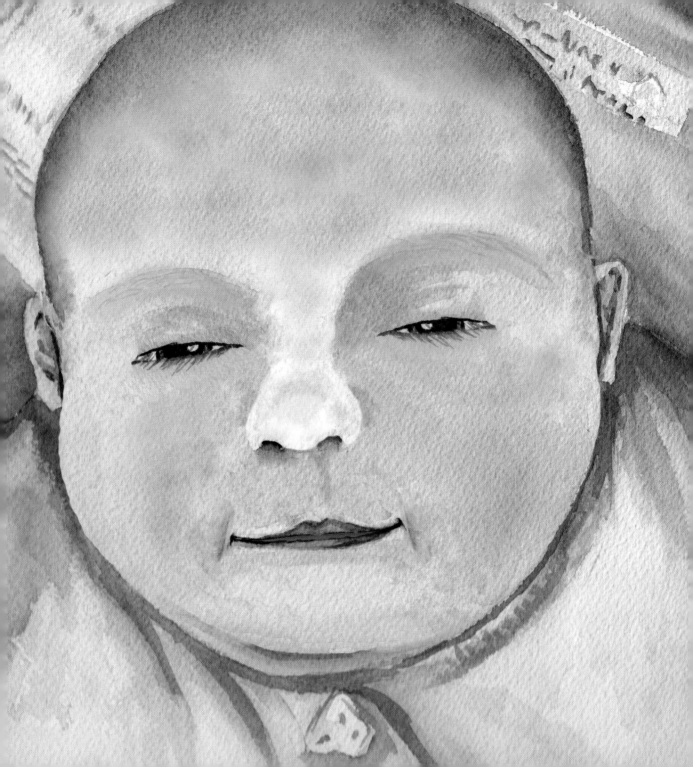

I gaze in wonder
at your round little face,
knowing this must be
God's most amazing grace.

I lift you to my shoulder
and breathe you in deep;
gently begin to sway
as you cuddle and sleep.

I listen to the rhythm of
your soft breath and coo -
suddenly there's nothing else
so important to do.

I move to our chair
in the glow of the night light,
feel the music wrap around us
and begin to rock you tonight.

I take it all in
and a small tear fills my eye,
as my love for you stops me,
and I let out a sigh.

I forget all the rest,
the chores and the tasks.
This love is so much more
than any mother could ask.

I drink in this moment,
and give thanks for this insight.
Whisper, "I love you, I love you,"
and rock you tonight.

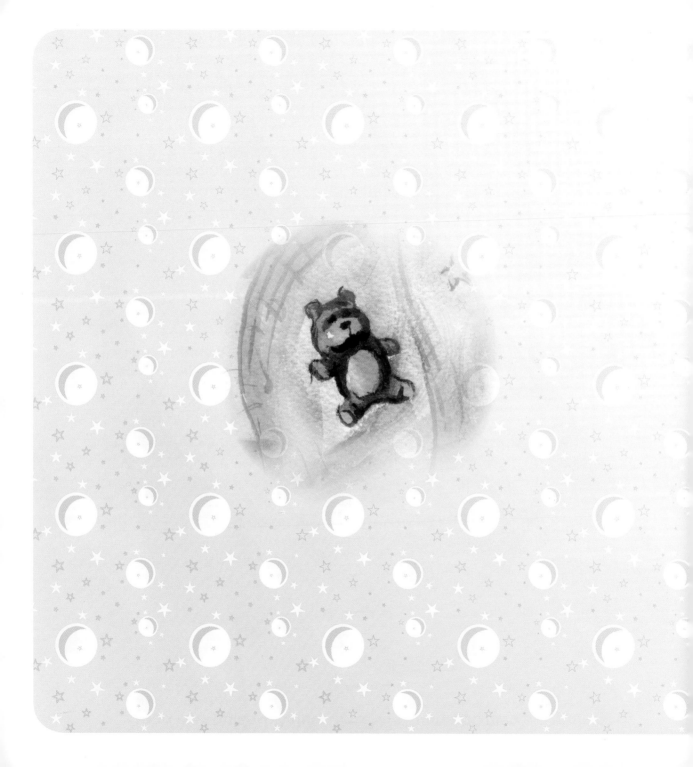

Author: Emily A. Roussell

Emily Roussell by profession is a speech-language pathologist. However, her most cherished role has become that of Mom to her young children. The words for this book came to her in the late evening hours she spent rocking her newborn twins. She and her husband, Michael, started Dream Big Publishing to put this lullaby to print and share it with others.

Illustrator: Chris Cooley

Chris Cooley began his journey toward becoming a designer at the age of two when he drew his first illustration of a whale on a bank deposit slip. He graduated from Syracuse University with a degree in Industrial and Interactive design and spent the next three years working at Cornell University as a graphic and web designer. In 2008 he decided to satisfy his life long dream of starting his own company and CMCreative Design was born.